Poison Dart Frogs
Up Close

Carmen Bredeson

E Enslow Elementary

CONTENTS

WORDS TO KNOW

poison [POI zun]—Something that can hurt or kill an animal or person.

slime [SLYM]—Thick, soft, slippery matter.

tadpoles [TAD pohlz]—Baby frogs. They look like fish.

vocal sac [VOH kul sak]—Skin on the throat that can blow up like a balloon.

Parts of a Poison Dart Frog

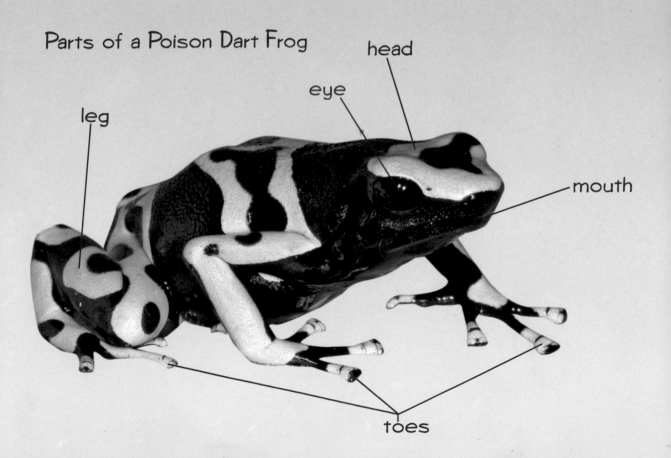

FROG HOMES

Poison dart frogs like warm, wet places. Some live high in trees in the rain forest. Others live near streams or rivers. These frogs are not very big. Some are as small as your thumbnail.

Poison dart frogs live in these shaded areas of South and Central America.

FROG SKIN

UP CLOSE

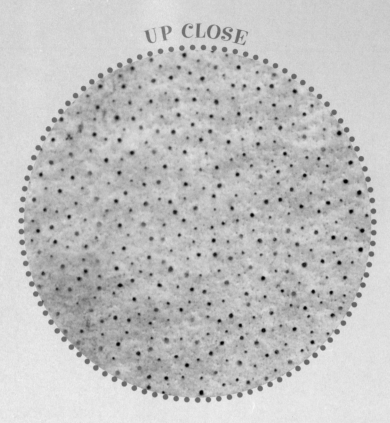

The skin of most poison dart frogs is bright
and colorful. Some frogs are red or purple.
Others are yellow, blue, or green. The bright
skin warns enemies to stay away!

FROG POISON

Ruby poison
dart frog

The **slime** on the frog's skin is a poison.
People in the rain forest dip their darts into
the slime. Then they use the poison darts to
kill animals for food. This is how the frogs
get their name.

The golden poison dart frog is the most poisonous of all poison dart frogs.

FROG VOCAL SAC

Phantasmal
(fan TAZ muhl)
poison frog

A male poison dart frog pushes air into
his **vocal sac**. The sac blows up like
a balloon. When the air comes out, the
sound is very loud. The call of a dart frog
sounds like a buzz or chirp.

Strawberry poison-dart frog ▶

10

FROG LEGS

Green and black
poison dart frog

A frog's back legs are longer than its
front legs. The back legs fold up when the
frog is sitting. They shoot straight out when
the frog jumps. Poison dart frogs do not
jump very far.

Amazonian (AM uh ZOH nee un) dart-poison frog ▶

FROG TOES

Dyeing black poison dart frog

Poison dart frogs crawl around on the forest floor. Sometimes they climb into the trees. The bottoms of their toes are sticky. The sticky toes keep the frogs from falling.

Rio Madeira (REE oh muh DAIR uh) poison frog ▶

14

FROG EGGS

A female poison dart frog lays 5 to 40 eggs at a time. She lays the eggs in a little puddle of water. Mother and father frogs stay near the eggs. In about two weeks, tiny **tadpoles** break out of the eggs.

Phantasmal poison frog with eggs ▶

16

FROG TADPOLES

UP CLOSE

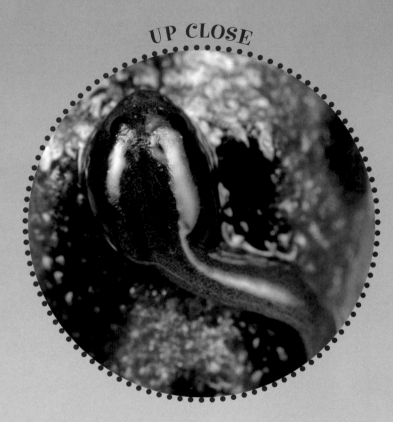

One of the parents backs up to the babies.

The tadpoles wiggle onto the parent's back.

Then the frog takes its babies to a pool of water.

The tadpoles swim away.

Red back poison frog ▶

LITTLE FROG

In a few weeks, the tadpole's tail starts to get smaller. Then it grows little legs and feet. The tadpole starts to look like a frog. The tiny frog leaves the water. It hops into the rain forest.

Blue poison dart frogs ▶

20

LIFE CYCLE

Eggs are laid in water.

Tiny tadpoles hatch in about 2 weeks.

Tadpoles turn into little frogs in 1 to 2 months.

Adult frogs have brightly colored skin.

◀ Green and black poison dart frog

LEARN MORE

BOOKS

Bishop, Nic. *Nic Bishop Frogs*. New York: Scholastic, 2008.

Satterfield, Kathryn. *Time for Kids: Frogs!* New York: Harper Collins Publishers, 2006.

Wechsler, Doug. *Poison Dart Frogs*. New York: PowerKids Press, 2002.

WEB SITES

All About Frogs
<http://www.kiddyhouse.com/themes/frogs/>

KidsKonnect
<http://www.kidskonnect.com/CONTENT/VIEW/32/27>

San Diego Zoo
<http://www.sandiegozoo.org/animalbytes/t-frog_toad.html>

INDEX

Series Literacy Consultant:
Allan A. De Fina, Ph.D.
Past President of the New Jersey Reading Association
Chairperson, Department of Literacy Education
New Jersey City University
Jersey City, New Jersey

Science Consultant:
Raoul Bain
Herpetology Biodiversity Specialist
Center for Biodiversity and Conservation
American Museum of Natural History
New York, NY

Note to Parents and Teachers: The **Zoom In on Animals!** series supports the National Science Education Standards for K–4 science. The Words to Know section introduces subject-specific vocabulary words, including pronunciation and definitions. Early readers may need help with these new words.

Enslow Elementary, an imprint of Enslow Publishers, Inc.
Enslow Elementary® is a registered trademark of Enslow Publishers, Inc.

Library of Congress Cataloging-in-Publication Data

Bredeson, Carmen.
  Poison dart frogs up close / Carmen Bredeson.
    p. cm. — (Zoom in on animals!)
  Summary: "Provides an up-close look at poison dart frogs for new readers"—Provided by publisher.
  Includes bibliographical references and index.
  ISBN-13: 978-0-7660-3077-0
  ISBN-10: 0-7660-3077-6
  1. Dendrobatidae—Juvenile literature. I. Title.
QL668.E233B74 2008
597.87'7—dc22   2007039467

Printed in the United States of America

10 9 8 7 6 5 4 3 2 1

To Our Readers: We have done our best to make sure all Internet Addresses in this book were active and appropriate when we went to press. However, the author and the publisher have no control over and assume no liability for the material available on those Internet sites or on other Web sites they may link to. Any comments or suggestions can be sent by e-mail to comments@enslow.com or to the address on the back cover.

Photo Credits: © 1999, Artville, LLC, p. 5; Art Wolfe/Photo Researchers, Inc., p. 1; © Barry Mansell/naturepl.com, p. 12; © George Bernard/Animals Animals, pp. 4–5; George Grall/Getty Images, p. 21; G.I. Bernard/Photo Researchers, Inc., p. 11; © iStockphoto.com/Lynda Roeller, p. 3; © Juergen & Christine Sohns/Animals Animals, p. 10; © Mark Moffett/Minden Pictures, pp. 6, 7, 9, 15, 18, 20; © Martin Harvey/Alamy, p. 14; © Michael and Patricia Fogden/Minden Pictures, p. 19; Michael Lustbader/Photo Researchers, Inc., p. 13; © Neil Bromhall/naturepl.com, p. 22 (top, left, and right); Olaf Leillinger, p. 22 (bottom); © Pete Oxford/naturepl.com, p. 17; Shutterstock, p. 8; Stephen J. Krasemann/Photo Researchers, Inc., p. 16.

Cover Photos: © Mark Moffett/Minden Pictures (left, top right); © Martin Harvey/Alamy (center right); Shutterstock (bottom right).

Back Cover Photo: © George Bernard/Animals Animals

Enslow Elementary
an imprint of
Enslow Publishers, Inc.
40 Industrial Road
Box 398
Berkeley Heights, NJ 07922
USA
http://www.enslow.com